# Postpartum Terror

By:
Kimberly Herzog

PublishAmerica
Baltimore

First printing

ISBN: 1-4241-3552-4
PUBLISHED BY PUBLISHAMERICA, LLLP
www.publishamerica.com
Baltimore

Printed in the United States of America

To my husband, Jeff.
Thank you for all your support.
Dedicated to our son, Noah.
We love you all the way to the moon and back.

# Acknowledgments

I want to thank the following people from the bottom of my heart and soul:

My husband, Jeffrey, for supporting me in this endeavor.

My son, Noah; without him there would be no book.

My dear friend Susan Gerometta who suggested I write this book in the first place.

My mother and father, Susan and Stephen Smith, who have always been there for me and encouraged me to do my best.

My brothers, Douglas and Brian Smith, who made me laugh every time I cried.

My dear friends Kevin Gough, Sharon O'Keefe, Jaime Pawelczak, Stacy Ramseyer, and Thomas English Winningham III, who listened with kind ears and hearts to all my fears and talked me through more than one potential panic attack.

Doctors Gordon, Yen and Risser and their entire staff for their excellent care and patience.

# About the Cover

One of the many responsibilities of motherhood is to send our children off to school with a healthy, albeit enjoyable lunch. A balance is achieved between nutritious and delicious. Most moms know if they go overboard on nutritious and skimp on delicious the lunch gets traded or dumped in the nearest garbage can. So every night mothers everywhere are carefully preparing lunches as their mothers did for them and so on back through time to the little red schoolhouse. My mother was very good at striking this balance and on Field Trip Days we got an extra special lunch. A larger brown bag with extra cookies and chips and drinks was always waiting for us on those mornings. Occasionally my dad would appear in the kitchen after we were in bed and tell my mom to go relax and he would make the lunches. After my mother gratefully left the kitchen in search of a hot bath and a good book my dad would begin the "SS Raid" of the kitchen. He managed to find every bit of sugary sweet and salty snack in the kitchen and stuff it in our bag. And to top it all off he gave us pop to drink! POP! Then he would carefully fold the bags and pull out his black magic marker. On the front of our lunch bags he would draw the picture you see on the cover. The next day when we saw that picture on our brown bags we knew it was going to be "A GOOD LUNCH TODAY!"

# Table of Contents

# Postpartum Terror

# Introduction

The new hot topic these days is postpartum depression. It is on the news, TV talk shows, books and magazines. However, no one talks about the flipside. The condition I lovingly refer to as Postpartum Terror. For those of you who are unsure what I mean allow me to explain. Postpartum Terror is the feeling that you cannot be out-of-range from your child for even a moment without cataclysmic consequences. Not to mention the fear that while you are in range you will do something to screw them up for life. Your fear and imagination do more than run wild, they go absolutely berserk. Terrifying events and occurrences that you never even considered in your whole life now seem not only possible, but probable. Many moms experience it. I know because when I mention it to other mothers I can see the mutual fear in their eyes. Through these discussions I have found out that I am not the only one who is concerned that my child could possibly choke on an errant eyelash or possibly scratch his eyeball and go blind if I do not immediately remove the "sleep crust" from his eyes.

Well, moms and dads, I have found no easy solution to make these fears go away. However, I have found that with a little support from those who love you, a little therapy, a little prayer, a little anxiety medication and a lot of humor it is possible to cope. Although I am able to laugh at the fears and "solutions" I have come up with during my first six months as a parent I am by no means cured. In fact I am reasonably sure that for every fear I conquer, two more will appear in its place.

When I was younger, I saw the movie *Psycho*. Mrs. Bates (Norman's mother) scared the hell out of me. Now I think perhaps she was just misunderstood. She just loved her son a little too much. It was at the moment of this epiphany that I realized I had to get a grip. I would hate it if twenty years from now my son said, "My mother was paranoid, over-protective and anxiety ridden. She never let me out of her sight, she never let me out of the house and she never let me do anything unsupervised....and that is why I killed all those women your honor." So in an effort to keep my son out of therapy, I have had to do some therapeutic practices of my own. Thus the book you are holding. However, be careful your child does not pick it up and get a paper cut. Those can be pretty nasty, especially if it gets infected. You would hate for them to lose a finger!

# Part One
## Water Games

# Chapter 1

In my current state of paranoia, the simplest task that I took for granted not so long ago has now become a race against time. Why? Because I cannot be away from my child for the normal amount of time it takes to go to the bathroom, much less shower.

After placing my son in his swing in front of his favorite television program, I run to take a shower. I have the door wide open and the shower curtain half way open. The reason for this is I do not know what kind of sound barrier a plastic shower curtain creates, but I am not taking any chances. I have just created a healthy shampoo lather when I hear my son gurgle. I leap from the shower, barely taking the time to grab a towel, and dash into the bedroom. My heart is in my throat as I am sure the sound I heard was my son trying in vain not to swallow his own tongue (although logically I know this is medically impossible). So here I stand dripping water and shampoo all over the carpet, while my son stares at me with a half grin on his face. Apparently he was just gurgling for the sake of gurgling.

# Chapter 2

I have always had a closed-door bathroom policy. I do not urinate well with others. Now I would not dream of closing the door. Instead I carry on some crazed bathroom conversation, yelling into the other room "Mommy is just peeing, I'll be right back sweetie!" As if he knows what that means. One night I had the flu and my husband, who is a firefighter/paramedic, was on shift. The baby and I were home alone. I was terrified he was going to wake up and need me while I was vomiting. I could not for the life of me figure out how I was going to handle it. So there I was, trying to muffle the sounds of illness. Have you ever tried to throw up silently. Well it ends up coming out your nose. Very unpleasant.

# Chapter 3

The only time I am ever really relaxed is the twenty minute to half hour baths I take when my husband is not on shift. I know he is in good hands with daddy and I can shut down my super-sonic mommy hearing. Well I can turn it down a bit at least. However, as soon as my son sounds fussy I get out of the tub as I am sure all hell is breaking loose. Usually I am just overreacting. Therefore my husband decides he is going to take our son for a walk so "mommy can truly relax". I had just stepped into a hot scented tub, my candles were lit, my classical music was playing softly and I was opening my newest library book when the bathroom door came bursting open. I half leap from the tub dripping water and bubbles to behold my husband, gasping for breath and cradling our screaming baby. "What happened?!?" I practically shriek.

"Nothing!" my husband practically shrieks back.

"Is he hurt or sick!?" I query truly starting to panic.

"No," my husband states flatly. It seems to be the only thing he is sure of. I wrap a towel around myself and take my son from my husband. He is not accepting any comfort (rubbing, shushing, rocking) so I sit down right there on the toilet, fortunately the lid was down and begin to breastfeed which at least brings some small measure of control to the situation. I look expectantly at my husband who is still standing there looking bewildered.

I ask again, "What happened?" I am much calmer as I can clearly see my son is not hurt.

"I do not know," my husband responds shaking his head. "Was he startled or frightened somehow? Was there a loud noise? Did he get hit with a sprinkler?" I ask in rapid succession. (Another explanation is required here. We had a pretty bad drought here this summer. Our village put a water ban on. For instance you can only water on odd/even days based on your address. So people wait until twilight to set out their sprinklers and do their bootleg watering as it is harder for the water police to spot. At any rate they overlap the sidewalk and timing them out can be tricky. Sometimes you get a bit misty.)

My husband's response to the sprinkler question is, "Yes, but that did not happen until later."

I look up at my husband blankly as I try to gauge if he is joking or not. Clearly he is not. I take a deep breath and advise him to do the same. Our son is calm, comforted and snuggled in his "happy place" (breast feeding) and all is quiet for the moment.

"OK, start from the beginning," I prompt. He takes another deep breath and begins. "We started on our walk and everything was fine. He was playing with his Froggy and cooing and I was talking along with him. It was such a nice evening and he seemed to be enjoying himself so I decided to take the long route. Well half way around the long block he starts screaming, I mean really freaking out! So I lift him out of the stroller to check him out and make sure he is not sick or in pain. He did not seem to have gas or any other pain and it did not look as if he had been bitten by any bugs or anything. There did not seem to be any reason for this episode so I just tried to comfort him. Well by this time people in their yards are starting to stare. They are looking at me kind of funny like I am abusing him or something. A few people look sympathetic, but most just looked suspicious. Of course, in retrospect I was probably just paranoid in my mortification. So I attempt to put him back in the stroller so we can head home. He was not having any of that. He all but roared at me. So I begin pushing the stroller in front of me with my left hand as I carry him in my right arm. Well I could not really steer that way so I switch him to my left and push with the right. This method is not working very well either. Especially when you are practically running. At this point neighbors are beginning to gather in their front yards to see what all the ruckus is about. I have never been so embarrassed in my life. I was so busy nodding and smiling to them in an effort to indicate that everything was OK that I never saw the sprinkler until it hit us full on. The screech that came out of our son practically split my eardrum. So I swung the stroller around and dragged it behind me while I half jogged/half stumbled home carry our screaming child the whole way."

In my own defense I would like to say that I had managed to keep a straight, if not sympathetic, face up until that point in the story. I burst out laughing. The kind of out of control laughter with tears. When I finally pulled myself together, I asked where the stroller was. He replied "I left it out front. As soon as I reached our property I abandoned ship and bolted for the door!" Suddenly he looked sheepish. "Oh, hey sorry about your bath."

"Oh don't worry about it," I chuckled, "that laugh was better than any bath I could ever take."

# Chapter 4

The first time I saw our son "stage a nutty", as I call it, was his first bath. As you know for the first two weeks or so, until the cord falls off baby gets a sponge bath. I believe I am the only mother in town who can honestly say that her son has an aversion to washcloths. He hates to have his face wiped off with a washcloth. Believe me there was no washcloth related trauma in his first couple hours or days of life and yet there it is. There it remains to this day as you will see as our story unfolds. At any rate the cord falls off and we are ready for our first bath. I should preface this by telling you that even during pregnancy baby bath time was something I was looking forward to. I was ready. We had a baby tub, towels, the dreaded washcloths, three different adorable terrycloth robes with matching slippers (yellow with ducks, green with an octopus and blue with a turtle.)

They were all so cute I could not choose just one so I registered for them all. I mean what if he found out there had been others and he did not have them? How upsetting for both of us. No, no, no it had to be done over my husbands strong objections I might add, we had every bath product known to man, three tub thermometers, tons of bath toys and of course the digital camera. I had literally dreamed of this moment. Our baby having fun and splashing about in the tub, what could be sweeter than that? Right? Wrong! He wigged out! The screaming and theatrics that ensued were enough to cause the neighbors to call the cops. Fortunately they did not. So there we are like a Marx Brothers skit, trying to get him lathered, rinsed and out of the water as quickly as possible. I think bathing a Saint Bernard may have been easier. It certainly would have been quieter and probably drier. We managed to get him cleaned, dried and dressed in record time, although it seemed like an eternity. I put him in his "happy place" and we have peace again. My husband is shaking his head and muttering "never again, sponge bath from now on until he is old enough to sit up in the tub."

# Chapter 5

Ladies and gentlemen I cannot stress enough that your greatest resource for these things is your mother. The Good Lord knows you will be getting plenty of advice from them about the things you do not want to discuss, so be smart enough to take advice on the things you will need help with. Swallow your pride, you do not know nearly as much as you think and you are not nearly as prepared as you hoped. By all means ask, beg if you must, for answers to some of the more complex things like. Why does my son scream in the tub like he is taking a hot lava bath? Is there a reason he screams and twists away from a washcloth as if it was covered in battery acid? Will he always stage a nutty when having to take his shirt off?

My mother, God bless her, has been a font of information. She told me about easing him in just to the waist in the sink and not his tub while leaving his t-shirt on. Thereby making him feel less vulnerable (see Part 3 entitled "Guilt" for more info on this). As for the washcloth she said "Well dear we all have our 'things'. He will grow out of it." Well he still has not but that is another story. As for the tub advice, it worked like a charm. Everyday we went a bit farther. Then we got him in the big tub with mommy and he has been having a ball ever since. However, bath time is still fraught with danger. I have already figured out how to get him out of the tub if for some reason I am going down. I have made sure there is an extra soft fluffy rug outside the tub in case I have to flip him over the side while I am losing consciousness. I would hate for him to break a bone or even get bruised but it is better than drowning. Then I started to wonder if my husband could install a high-speed drain that could empty the tub in a matter of seconds. Then instead of flipping my son I could flip a switch and even if we went down the water would be gone in seconds, not leaving enough time for a drowning. Unless of course he got his hand or foot caught in the drain and was unable to remove it due to the power of the suction. Then I could not flip him at all and the water level would remain. "Time to get out of the tub!! Let's Go! Let's GO!" On the bright side the adorable playing and splashing during bath time that I had dreamed of has become a reality. Now he gets annoyed when it is time to get out of the tub.

# Chapter 6

In fact he enjoys the water so much that when we went to my mother-in-law's house in Florida for our vacation he went in the pool and loved it. He was three months old at the time. Of course he owned two bathing suits, a beach towel, sunglasses, pool shoes and a sun hat. So there we are on the screened patio, next to the in-ground indoor/ outdoor pool. The sun is filtered through the screen but I still slathered enough sunscreen on him to spend an afternoon on the equator. The water is bath water warm but I still make sure he is warm enough by constantly checking his body temperature and only allowing five minutes of swimming at a time before taking him out of the pool, taking off his wet bathing suit, drying him off, putting him in dry clothes, putting his suit in the dryer so he can go back in the pool in half an hour for another five minutes. But it was worth it. He loved it and did what I call his Ballet of the Sea Frog. Daddy held him under his arms while baby held his head up and back, threw his arms straight back and let his legs float out behind him like a frog. It was priceless. He had the time of his life. I on the other hand was a nervous wreck. I would not let any of the other cousins in the water while he was in the pool as I was afraid he would get splashed, I kept telling my husband told hold him higher as his chin would occasionally touch water and God forbid he get wet-chin, which could lead to other various things that I do not know about, but imagine can be pretty bad. However, this was a high water mark for me as I allowed him in the pool for one thing and for another I let him out of my mother-vise-grip long enough for other adults in the family to play with him in the pool. But of course where would our pool adventure be without at least one irrational fear. My gaze is drawn to the pool filter. I start to wonder if it can suddenly go into over-drive and suck in my baby's foot or arm as he floats by causing a serious aquatic injury. Or even worse, don't they have huge alligators down here? They are pretty quick too. If one of them busted through the screen doors or windows and made a beeline for the pool could I get my son out in time? OK, EVERYONE OUT OF THE POOL!

# Part 2

## Putting the Baby to Bed

(Wherever That May Be)

# Chapter 7

One of the biggest challenges I have had is definitely bedtime. Through no fault of my son's who has slept through the night since he was one month old. Even throughout the first month he only got up once a night for a feeding. No the fault rests entirely upon my shoulders. It was my fear. Fear of the Angel of Death who comes in the night without rhyme or reason. Dare I name him? Shall we call him SID for short? There are so many theories about Sid and why he comes and what we can do to keep him at bay. I watch my son like a hawk as I understand a baby is not completely out of the woods on this one until their second birthday. For the first four months I had him in the master bedroom with us. Not in our bed of course because they say that is a big no-no and draws Sid to your home. They say the dangers of him being tangled up and/or rolled over on are too great. My husband and I purchased a bassinet for our son and set it up right next to our bed on my side. I must have felt for his breathing every fifteen minutes all night long. Eventually I worked up to forty-five minutes. I was able to accomplish this thanks to my son who is a very loud sleeper. He makes all kinds of noises and sighs in the night, which let mommy know he is just fine. Unfortunately, the noises unnerve daddy. He thought that every noise was to be followed by an awakening. Therefore he slept on edge for a while. I on the other hand was grateful for the noises, as it was the only thing that helped me sleep. Whenever I woke up and was about to roll over and put my hand upon his chest he would sigh and save me the roll. I would peacefully drift off for another forty-five minutes. Make no mistakes, it was not real sleep, but a pseudo-mommy-sleep. The kind where Mommy can feel, hear, see and smell everything while giving off the appearance of sleep. On the third night home we were all asleep the baby in his bassinet on my right and I facing him, my husband on my left rolled to face my back. During the night he went to roll over on his other side and in my pseudo-mommy-sleep I mistook him for the baby. My arm shot out like the bionic woman and grabbed his hip holding him in place. He tried in vain to roll over but I held fast afraid he would fall. He finally woke up and woke me up asking “What are you doing?!?” I let go, apologizing.

“I am sorry I thought you were the baby and I was afraid you were going to fall out of bed. Go back to sleep. Sorry.”

# Chapter 8

Several nights later my husband had a bit of a coughing fit in the middle of the night. He managed to muffle it pretty well. It woke me up and the baby too but not completely. It was one of those things where you know something woke you but are unsure of what it was. Well I figured since I am awake I'll do a chest check. Well as I mentioned the baby was half awake as well so when I touched him I scared the poor thing within an inch of his life. He began screaming to beat the band. There was no consoling him. So it is back to the happy place for baby where he quietly drifted back to sleep. No drifting for us, we lay there feeling guilty for an hour.

# Chapter 9

I remember reading about being careful not to put foreign objects in the bed with your baby, as they can be dangerous. I thought, *Are you kidding? I did not need to be told that!* I practically nailed the fitted crib sheet to the mattress for fear that it would suddenly become loose and somehow get itself lodged in his throat! I allowed him to fall asleep with his snuggly elephant blanket and basically sat on the edge of my bed staring at him until it was time to take it away. The books also talk about the dangers of the baby becoming to warm in the middle of the night. That this rolls out the red carpet for Sid. So I began what I call the "Blanket Shuffle." I start out with a blanket appropriate for the temperature of the room, the temperature of his body and the type of pajamas he is wearing. I leave a supply of blankets nearby. These blankets are of varying thickness and material. At each hourly interval I reassess the situation and re-adjust the blanket coverage accordingly. My husband says I look like one of those street card hustlers. Where is the baby? Now you see him now you don't! Which blanket is he under?

Pick the right one and win a prize!! Another frightening discovery has been that although it was recommended for years that babies be put to bed on their stomachs to avoid choking on spit-up. It now may be the number one cause for Sid to drop by unannounced. The problem with this is that he is eating cereal and baby food now. I am terrified that he will vomit up the food and choke. I wasn't as worried about breast milk and formula as he would turn his head and dribble it out. But solid food? Don't they always tell you that when putting your drunk friend to bed after his burrito turn him on his side or stomach so he doesn't choke on his own vomit? Is a baby so much more advanced that I need not worry? It is all very confusing. So these are the things I lay in bed think about and listen for. I remember when I was pregnant I had horrible insomnia. I asked my OB/GYN when this would go away. He said, "Right about the time they move out." Somehow, in retrospect I do no think he was kidding.

# Chapter 10

As I mentioned in part one we went on vacation when he was three months old to visit my sister-in-law Jennifer. Jennifer has been an island of sanity in my sea of psychotic fear and has helped me more than I can ever thank her for. We stayed a few days with Jennifer and her family and then we all headed to my mother-in-law's home. We took along our pack-n-play, which by the way is a wonderful, must own product. It is a crib, changing table, play pen all rolled into one small easily packed easily set up package, complete with light, mobile, sound machine and lullabies. This is the bed my baby slept in for the duration of our trip. Of course I carefully positioned it next to me. However, there was a dilemma. As we were in Florida, literally every bedroom has a ceiling fan. A CEILING FAN?! Is that thing screwed in tightly enough? Could it come loose in the night? What if just one blade falls off? Or the whole thing comes out of the ceiling plunging into my son's crib? What are the blades made of? Could it kill him on impact or just cause a dangerous aerial accident? I turn to my husband. "OK help me move this out from under the fan. Better yet turn the fan off I do not know how far one of those blades can fly if dislodged. I am no physics expert. I do not care how nice the breeze feels, the air conditioner is enough. Besides I do not have enough time to set up a whole new spare blanket configuration based on the addition of a ceiling fan."

# Chapter 11

A pack-n-play is substantially bigger than a bassinet. My son discovered this in his sleep in a matter of nights. During my many middle of the night checks, I realized that my son was slowly turning clockwise. Not to mention flailing his arms and legs with apparent abandon and much needed freedom. By the time we got home I knew he was too big for the bassinet and that it was time for his own crib. Much to the joy of my husband who had been trying to make this happen for some time now, my mother and mother-in-law who had been asking me during every conversation we had in the last two months if the baby was in his crib yet. However, this turn of events was breaking my heart, which by the way was now in my throat with fear. Not only because I could not be in the room with him, simply a roll over away in case of emergency. But I would not be next to him if he simply needed his mommy for comfort. I was furious with everyone who pressured me to "Put him in his crib" before I was ready, including my husband. Especially my husband because I was sure he had recruited the others in his cause.

Then I heard about “the monitor”. I met a woman at a seminar who told me about an amazing monitor that was so sensitive that it measured the baby’s movement, breathing included right through the mattress!!! I AM SAVED!!! So I told my husband I would move the baby as soon as I had the monitor. He said, “Great, when will that be?”

I replied with a smile, “As soon as I can get it shipped here from Israel.” His jaw dropped at this, but God love him he ordered it and had it shipped over for me. On the day he was to move into the crib I was beside myself. My husband was teaching a night class of EMT students and I was home alone putting him to bed. I called my brothers hysterical. I was not ready. My brother Doug came through with better and kinder reasoning than anyone else had.

He said, “You did such a beautiful job decorating his nursery. Everything you did was with his happiness and comfort in mind. You would hate for him to miss out on that wouldn’t you?” My brother had hit home with that. He was right and he wasn’t pressuring me with the standard party line everyone else was using about how the baby needed to be in his own room on his own to develop. He spoke from the heart directly to mine. I looked around the nursery and realized how hard I had tried to make it a warm and nurturing place. I would hate for him to be too old to enjoy it by the time he came in here. My brother Doug gave me the courage to do what needed to be done that night. Don’t get me wrong, I slept on the floor of the nursery, right next to his crib. But, he slept in the nursery in his own crib that night and has ever since.

# Chapter 12

I only sleep in the nursery once in a while if he is sick or particularly distraught. There have been very few false alarms from the monitor. They only occur if he rolls to a corner of the crib and off the monitor or I accidentally move the monitors askew when changing his sheets. Let me tell you when it does go off it will stop your heart. Especially because it does not cause my son to awaken. It should as it is as loud as a smoke detector and it is coming from his crib, however he does not even stir. This is made even stranger by the fact that we can tip toe past his room for a glass of water and he is instantly awake peeking at you from between his crib slats. Yet this insanely loud beeping does not even cause him to flinch which is terrifying when you run in there because he may not be breathing and instead of him crying out in fear he is laying there motionless, still asleep and I have to feel his chest to be sure he is all right while my husband is frantically trying to shut down the alarm before it actually scares our son breathless which is why we are standing here in the first place. All in all, the monitor is one of the best investments I have ever made. I actually sleep for an hour or two at a time instead of a mere forty-five minutes. Unfortunately, the monitor cannot stop an over-active imagination. Nighttime is the worst. The ideas that can come to mind in the wee hours are insane. I remember one night thinking to myself, *I wonder if spontaneous combustion is really possible. Maybe I should get him a couple sets of those flame retardant pajamas. But if they are flame resistant and he bursts into flames from the inside wouldn't that just seal the fire in?! Oh for the love of heaven I am never going to get to sleep now! That's just great! Wait, what was that sound? Did that sound like a crackling noise? I don't smell anything. Of course my sinuses are pretty bad. I better go check just to be sure.*

# Chapter 13

There is also the fear of kidnapping. Now I am here to tell you that with the baby monitors we have today, I could hear a pin drop, much less someone sneaking into his room. (As a side-note this would be a great device for parents of teenagers who sneak out at night. Hide a monitor under the bed and they won't even get the latch open without you hearing it.) The point is there is no way someone can enter that room without me knowing it, but one night I heard a strange ticking sound. I thought for sure some master kidnapper had cut a hole in my son's window and was gently tapping the glass out. As it turns out the master criminal was his "Winnie the Pooh" wall clock, but it never hurts to check.

# Chapter 14

My final ditch effort to keep Sid at bay is the bed charms: a cradle medal, a miniature crucifix with a silver heart bearing my sons named and Mexican protection bracelet that I pinned to the crib skirting. I do not know what Sid is afraid of, but I am not fooling around here. If anyone has a Tibetan Good Luck charm they would like to send me I am not above using it.

# Part 3
## Guilt
(Starting a Therapy Trust Fund For Your Child)

# Chapter 15

An emotion that goes hand-in-hand with parental fear is parental guilt. Guilt leads to the fear that we will ruin our child's psyche and cause them to require extensive therapy someday. Thus, the starting of the Therapy Trust Fund (TTF). There are two different sub-sections to this guilt. The first type is the category I call "the things we imagine". The second category I call "the mistakes we actually make".

Let us begin with the first category—"the things we imagine." What I mean by this is that the normal things we are supposed to do or must do as parents can still make us feel guilty. For example, I feel guilty putting my son in his rear facing car seat and going anywhere that takes more than a five-minute drive. So I spend the entire time chattering away at him and singing along with his music because I am afraid he will feel abandoned if I don't. Although he is perfectly content to look out the window and watch the world outside go by. Every time I look in the mirror at him through his mirror I feel like those little eyes are accusing me of leaving him alone. So my husband and

I broke down and bought the DVD player for the car. I feel much better knowing he is able to watch his favorite movies on extensive car trips (fifteen minutes in duration or longer). I must admit I still talk to him, but only every three to five minutes or so instead of that constant stream of chatter he used to get. Plus I put some money in his TTF after every long trip.

# Chapter 16

Every time I have to put him in his swing, bouncy chair, sit 'n' play or play mat I feel awful. Even though I only do it in order to throw in some laundry, heat up a supplement for him, warm his baby food or cook the family dinner. If I continue with the housework I will be broke and his TTF will hit the million-dollar mark by his eighteenth birthday. I do not set him down for my own leisure but that does not stop the guilt. Unfortunately my son now knows this. His answer to this dilemma is the screech. It is not crying or continuous screaming. It is a short ululating blast that could make your ears bleed. A trait he inherited from his uncle Brian who can screech like a banshee on a foxhunt. My brother Brian developed this screech as a child and although he is twenty-seven years old, I believe he can still do it. The stories of Brian and that screech could fill a whole separate book. At any rate our bouncing baby boy has that particular family talent in his treasure trove. He uses it wisely, when he feels he is not getting the attention he deserves or when he is really angry about something. Where as uncle Brian always used it to amuse himself and scare the living daylights out of my parents. Brian always managed to find the darkest and quietest places too let one out. As I said the stories could fill their own book. My son also has a showman type flair for the dramatic and in addition to the screech developed a fake cough that can be quite effective.

# Chapter 17

There were certain things that made my son scream bloody murder. Number one....the dreaded washcloth. It did not bother him when having his body washed, but heaven forbid you use one on his face. This is still an issue. He has expanded his distaste to napkins, paper towels, burpy cloths and any other item one might use to remove cereal, formula, drool or spit up from his face. The worst part of this is that I try to reason with him saying things like, "Mommy does not allow dirty faces,"; "You must be clean,"; "A gentleman is never sloppy;" or "I do not like your tone dear." He just looks at with a half grin as I have stopped wiping his face in order to make these ridiculous statements therefore in effect he has won. There was the diaper and clothing change screaming fit. This went on for the first two months or so. Every time my husband or I started to change his diaper or clothing he went into a rage. Apparently this was an unacceptable practice in his eyes. He expressed his displeasure with a longer version of the screech. It ran the full length of time the changing required. My husband and I felt horrible. We discussed it at length. It seems he is afraid of being undressed in anyway. Even a change of socks or booties was distressing to him. So we began our own nursery version of beat the clock. Like an *I Love Lucy* skit we attempt to tag team change his diaper and/or clothes as quickly as possible. Our background music...The Opera of the Slaughtered Screech Monkey performed by our son. Finally I realized our own sense of guilt was making a bad situation worse. So I suggested we do this one at a time in a slower but efficient pace and we will just put more money in his the TTF. The TTF is up 10% at the close of nursery business today.

# Chapter 18

One day we were at my parents house and my husband was cleaning out my son's nose. He said look it is a bit discolored. I wonder if he is getting a cold or sinus infection. So of course we took his temperature, checked his ears, nose and throat, and watched him closely throughout the day. Thank goodness we did not call a doctor. It was at dinner that I realized what was wrong with our son. As I watched him eating or shall we call it playing with a swallow at the end I realized what he had. He did not have a cold or a sinus infection. He had SQUASH! That is correct! a dreaded case of SNS. In all his playing around he managed to get baby food up his nose. Well, that is my professional mommy diagnosis Squash-Nose Syndrome.

# Chapter 19

In an effort to make hygeine more fun for him, I put on his music and talk and sing to him. This seemed to be working, especially once I started making up songs for our get ready tasks. There are now songs for...booties/socks/shoes, lotion (one song for night time lotion and one for regular baby lotion), a diaper cream song and a baby powder song. My husband was not to be outdone by these songs. One day before nap time my husband took my son into the nursery to change his diaper. Suddenly I heard my husband doing his own rendition of the theme from *Mission Impossible.* Upon their return my husband proudly stated that my son had successfully received his mission. According to my husband, the mission statement was in the diaper and had to be received and placed in the diaper pail in thirty seconds before self-destruct. I turned to my son and queried "What is your mission should you choose to accept it?" My husband answering on my son's behalf said in a small, but proud voice "I have to take a nap!"

# Chapter 20

The morning diaper change remained an ordeal for quite sometime. Gratefully we are past it now. But for months every morning it was the same thing. I would do our wake up routine, making a big deal of the process of course. Welcoming my son into a brand new day is one of the highlights of our day. Until I lift him out of the crib and place him on the changing table. Then the hysterics begin he would scream and cry in protest as he felt a feeding should come first. I tried in vain to explain to him that I do not allow dirty diapers at breakfast or any other meal for that matter, but he did not seem to understand much less care. I even went so far as to tell him that "A gentleman never screeches! Except for your uncle Brian, but that is a story for another day." However, now I think he finally understands that there will be food immediately following the pamper change. It is not an either/or situation. Thank goodness, that was at least a buck every morning in the TTF.

# Chapter 21

One time I was a bit over-zealous with the powder and it caused us both to cough. I felt so bad. Anyone who tells you that the child is too young too be effected by these things much less remember them has never met my child. Ever since the "powder incident" every time I pull out the powder and start the song he lets out one of his fake coughs and then laughs at me. I have since taken that particular dollar back from the TTF!! He has used that cough many times to his advantage. In the beginning he hated to have formula supplements in between breast feedings. So every time you put the bottle in his mouth he did the fake cough/gagging bit. It is enough to scare you half to death. You flip him forward and start patting him on the back as he watches you from the corner of his eye with that smirk on his face. However, it worked every time because we were afraid that the one time we ignored it he would really be choking. He wins again. Fortunately he enjoys his bottles now so we don't have to do our four times daily Heimlich anymore. During these bottle feedings he also employs his other secret weapon...The

Screech. He does not like to be burped half way through and screams for all he is worth until the burp comes out. Now we have two different guilt feelings at battle...The guilt of pulling a bottle from the mouth of a hungry (starving to hear him tell it) baby or the guilt of our baby getting a tummy ache because he was not burped half way through his bottle. The latter won out so now my husband and I are both deaf in one ear from his not so subtle protests of our decision. Of course then I am trying to calmly reason with him and explain our "tummy ache reasoning". I do not think he is listening. Ah, guilt what fun! Oh well, another dollar in the TTF.

# Chapter 22

The fake cough is a stitch. When a child is young they do a bit of light coughing. I do not know why. Maybe they are clearing things out a bit or just stretching and expanding their respiratory system. Yet, every time my son would cough I would come running.

After seeing that he was all right, I would pat his chest or back and say, "Oh my, that was a big cough for a little pumpkin." Well, it did not take my son long to figure out that every time he let out a little fake cough I would come running. So now he uses it constantly to get me to come to him. I feel like one of Pavlov's dogs. Although I guess it is better than screaming and crying for attention as many babies do. He can be in his swing, his chair, his father's lap it does not matter.

If I dare to walk past without acknowledging him, which is very rare, he lets out a little cough as if to say, "Mommy I need you." And of course I run over and give him the pat and the party line.

My husband thinks this is hilarious. "Boy does he have your number!" he laughs at me. But let me say that it is worth it just to get that baby toothless smile at the end of our little cough routine.

# Chapter 23

The next category is for the mistakes we actually make. While on vacation I attempted to clip my son's finger nails. Unfortunately his travel clippers were bigger and a bit more awkward than the ones I usually use at home. I accidentally clipped a bit of his skin. I did not cut it off, but I did cut into him a bit. His eyes widened with shock, he threw his other arm back and began to scream. I scooped him up and tried to comfort him while apologizing over and over. The histrionics that followed were ridiculous. Not him, me. He stopped crying after a minute and went to his happy place. I on the other hand cried for a full ten minutes. I sat there holding my son and sobbing. My husband was holding me comforting and cooing the way he does with our son in a kind effort to console me. "Look he is not even crying anymore. He is not bleeding either, it isn't even as deep as a paper cut. You barely nicked him."

"It doesn't matter," I sobbed, "I hurt our baby." I did not think I could ever clip his nails again. However, I realized that if I did not finish the job right then and there, I would never have the courage to do it again. This would give my son the ability to scale bamboo trees by his first birthday. That would definitely be worse and far more dangerous. So I calmed down and finished the job. Then I went out and bought the baby nails scissors and an “I am sorry I clipped you” gift. Plus a fiver in the FUND. I am a good one for guilt gifts. After every doctor’s appointment he gets an “I-got-shots-today” gift. Guilt is getting to be pretty expensive.

# Chapter 24

One other incident comes to mind. One night in the first two weeks our baby was home he awoke in the middle of the night. He was not crying as he did not really do that, but he was awake, or so I thought. I lifted him from his crib and began carrying him to the nursery for a diaper change. On the way to the nursery he really did wake up and was terrified to realize he was in motion and in the dark. He began screaming and it took a bit of time to calm him down. That may have been the night I started the TTF.

# Chapter 25

Fortunately I have had no major accidents with him. No falls, no drops, no running into things with the baby. Knock on wood. I did fall out of the rocking chair with him once, but I protected him and took the entire brunt of it myself. OK I can see this needs an explanation as well. How does one fall out of a rocking chair? Was I really going that fast? NO. I was feeding my son and rocking him to sleep. Well I started the blanket shuffle and decided he needed a warmer one than the one he was currently wrapped in. There was one behind me so I scooched to the edge of the chair to pull it out from behind me. Well apparently it was also underneath me. I gave it a tug and jacked myself right out of the chair. My husband and his sister were in the living room. They said I hit the floor so hard that they both thought something had hit the house and ran out the front door in search of what or who had made the sound. Upon finding nothing they returned to the house to hear our son crying. Not in pain as he did not get hurt or even bumped. However, he was half asleep so the fall startled him. My poor husband came running into to the nursery to find his wife and son on the floor. Not a good moment in his life.

# Part 4
## Miscellaneous Fears, Quirks, and Irrational Moments

# Chapter 26

I would like to start this chapter by saying that I did speak to a professional about my fears. It was my six-week post delivery exam with my OB/GYN who is wonderful. I explained that I lived with a constant sickening fear that something would happen to my child. I was actually in tears by the time I finished explaining the way my imagination runs away with itself. I mean I could not watch the news, nor could I watch my favorite television dramas because of the fears the violence would instill in my heart. I could not even talk to my husband about his job. One day he was telling me about a fifty-five year old patient who had died. I burst into tears. My husband was taken completely off guard.

"What on earth is wrong with you?" he asked.

"That was somebody's son!" I sobbed in response.

My husband looked intently at me and said, "Perhaps you should talk to a doctor about this."

"I have an appointment this Friday," I sniffled. I admit it, I am afraid of the tragic accident, the freak accident, the unbelievable, horrifying things that can happen, things that no one can foresee. Thus the name "freak/tragic accident". It makes perfect sense to me.

After I finished explaining all of this to my doctor he was very kind a sympathetic. He asked if I was depressed at all. I replied, "I am not depressed, I am terrified. I do not even like to leave the room he is in for a second because I am afraid something awful will happen." He suggested something for anxiety and counseling. I said I could not take anything that would be harmful while breast feeding or that would deaden my heightened, tightly strung, fox like alertness.

He assured me he would never prescribe such a thing. At the close of our appointment he turned to me and carefully said, "If you feel suicidal please call me immediately."

I was stunned, my jaw literally dropped. "Suicide!" I gaped at him. "Are you kidding me? I just told you I was afraid to leave the room. What makes you think I would be willing to leave the planet?! Boy are you barking up the wrong tree. That is not even in my personality. Besides who would take care of him?" My voice was rising by this time as I was starting to imagine what would happen to my poor baby if I were dead. My poor doctor is more like it. God bless him!

He calmly said, "I was not implying that you would do such a thing but I have to ask."

# Chapter 27

Apparently my official diagnosis is postpartum anxiety. However, I do not think the word "anxiety" paints the picture of raw fear as vividly as postpartum "terror". This terror began the day he was born. The overwhelming love coupled with fear for his well-being left me breathless. I immediately had my brother-in-law Michael, who is a minister, bless him right over the phone. As I was in a Catholic hospital, I asked a priest to come in and do a blessing as well. I would have invited a rabbi, a shaman and a high priest of Isis to participate too, but I did not know any. COVER ALL YOUR BASES!

# Chapter 28

There is nothing a mother would not do to protect her young. Your fears of other things evaporate, when your fear for their safety arises. One day I was pushing my son around the block in his stroller. Two dogs I had never seen before come tearing around the corner teeth bared barking like the Hounds of Hell. I had a split second of fear that they would leap for the carriage. Then I remember that they could smell fear so I let the rage take over. I turned and took a menacing step toward the dogs, putting myself between them and the baby. I yelled "GET BACK!" with all the venom and force of a mother protecting her young. Both dogs came to a dead halt. They stared at me, apparently saw a look in my eyes that told them I would use my own fangs to do some throat ripping and they turned and ran away.

DO NOT MESS WITH THE MAMA!

# Chapter 29

A bit if advice about babysitters: choose one whose biological clock is ticking. Trust me on this. Find a woman in her late twenties or early thirties who is dying for a child of her own. It was easy for me to spot her, as I was that woman until I had my son. She is wonderful with my son and the best part is I know she is holding him the entire time I am gone. Not much can happen to your baby while he is being snuggled and adored can it?

The Good Book says, "Love thy neighbor." Well this book says I have discovered an ability to hate my neighbors with the heat of a nova. Most of my neighbors are delightful. Yet there are always a few inconsiderate ones aren't there? You know the ones. Every sporting event, holiday, or weekend night where the booze abounds the entire block must be aware of their presence and intoxication. It does not happen often but when it does I lay there seething in white-hot rage. Swearing to the Lord above that if they wake my son there will be hell to pay. The anger I feel at the moment surprises even me. It does not last as even if I seem them the next day I just let it go.

But at the moment if I had an annihilate button I would press it in a heartbeat. Not that waking my son is a crime. But if the noise frightens him in anyway there will be payback and it will be unpleasant.

# Chapter 30

One night I jump out of bed and run in to the living room to inform my husband that I have solved all of our problems and worries as to where we should raise our son. Deep sigh as he turns from the computer to look at me. He is used hearing “another one of my really great ideas” on a regular basis, especially at night.

I smile and proudly state, “We are moving to AMISH COUNTRY!” My husband continues to look at me impassively so I take that as my cue to continue. “Think about it. When is the last time you heard about an attack of any kind, murder, or kidnapping in Amish Country? Never! There is no drunk driving as they do not drink or drive much less simultaneously. Have you ever heard of a nationwide manhunt for an Amish Serial Killer! I think not! It is brilliant!”

My husband blinks and asks calmly, “Aren’t you forgetting something?”

“What?” I challenge.

My husbands replies blandly, “He could be the victim of a tragic farming accident.” It is my turn to blink. I hadn’t thought of that. I turn on my heel and head back to the bedroom. I just can’t win.

# Chapter 31

Finally I must say to my parents that my understanding of their actions in our upbringing is so very crystal clear now. I used to laugh, roll my eyes and/or get just plain annoyed at their fears for our well-being. Oh do I get it now. My father, God love him, still thinks I should be safely at home when the street lights come on. I am thirty-seven years old, a wife and mother. That does not matter. What does matter is that I am still his baby. A visit to my parents usually ends in the following fashion. After a few hours my dad starts to do clock watch. In the spring and summer there is more leeway as it gets dark later. But in the autumn and winter this ritual starts between 2:00 pm and 2:30 pm. He looks at the clock and then at me and says, “You better get going.”

I raise my eyebrows. “Why are we annoying you?”

“No, of course not but it is getting late,” he says.

“Dad, it is only 2:15 pm,” I reply.

“I know that,” he explains with a sigh. “But, if you do not leave now you will get caught in traffic, then a fifty-minute drive will become a two hour drive. If that happens it will be dark out by the time you get home." I used to argue with this, explaining that in the twenty-one years I have been driving, much of it has been in the dark. However, now I just smile, pack up, and kiss him good-bye. Of course I call him as soon as I walk in the door so he knows I made it home safe.

# Chapter 32

Thank you Mom and Dad for teaching me how to be a good parent. Thank you my darling little brothers Doug and Brian for teaching me how to be silly with little boys. Thank you to the four of you for listening to my fears. Reassuring me when needed, advising whether I knew I needed or not and laughing with me as I laughed at myself. Thank you to my dear friends Sue, Sharon, and Jeff—who is also my husband—for listening, laughing, and telling me to "Write this stuff down, it will make a great book someday." Thank you to my darling son for taking me on this fun and terrifying ride. Thank you to my husband for helping me create an addition to this crazy family I call home. Thank you to you, dear reader, for taking this journey with me. I hope this brought you many laughs and only the kinds of tears that come with a good laugh. I hope you know that you are not alone. I hope you realize that the postpartum depressants are not the majority. The postpartum paranoids win by a landslide. A landslide?! I never thought about a landslide, or any other natural disaster for that matter. Oh no! If you will excuse me I have to go check the foundation of my house. Not to mention the structural sturdiness around the nursery!